REACHING MIDDLE SCHOOL READERS

ISBN 0-618-06875–9

3 4 5 6 7 8 9 – BHV – 04 03 02 01

Table of Contents

Table of Contents

One of the many challenges of middle school teaching is accommodating the wide range of reading abilities and interests among students. For those students who are hooked on reading, the challenge is to provide a steady diet of rich materials. But for many students, reading is a chore that requires enormous effort and yields little success.

Students who are not able to read at grade level often do not succeed in school. While much of the focus of the early grades is on learning to read, the focus shifts in the middles grades to reading to learn. Students who do not have a strong foundation in basic decoding and comprehension skills become struggling readers. Their poor reading ability denies them access to the content of the textbooks; as a result, they fall behind in almost every subject area. Below-level reading ability most often is the result of inadequate decoding skills, poor comprehension, or a combination of both.

Decoding skills provide readers with strategies for figuring out words that are unfamiliar in print but are part of their speaking vocabulary. Basic decoding skills involve matching letters and letter combinations with spoken sounds and blending those sounds into words. As students encounter longer— multisyllabic— words, they need to divide these words into manageable chunks or syllables.

Decoding is an enabling skill for comprehension. Comprehension is a process of constructing meaning from text. Readers integrate the information in the text with their prior knowledge to make sense of what they read. Specific comprehension skills and strategies, such as main idea, sequence, and visualizing, can help students recognize the relationships among ideas, figure out text structures, and create pictures of what they read.

This book provides some basic tools and strategies that will help you help your students to become readers. The lessons and articles can be used as needed, or they can be organized into mini-units of instruction.

Developing Fluency in All Readers

Reading fluency is the ability to automatically recognize words so that attention can be focused on the meaning of the written material. Fluency involves both decoding and comprehension skills; fluent readers decode text with little or no effort as they construct meaning from that text. Teachers can usually spot readers who struggle with decoding the text. Other readers, however, may be able to say the words and sound as though they are reading, but they have little or no understanding of what they read. These readers often go unnoticed, especially in the content areas.

Fluency is a developmental skill that improves with practice. The more students read, the better readers they become. The reading level at which a student is fluent is called his or her *independent reading level*. However, a student's independent reading level may vary with the type of material he or she is reading. For example, reading a short story is often easier than reading a textbook.

A key part in developing reading fluency is determining a student's independent reading level and then providing a range of materials at that level. Chapter 1 offers diagnostic tools for determining reading levels, tips for improving fluency, and a listing of books at various reading levels.

Helping All Readers Break the Code

There are many reasons that some students struggle with reading. Often poor readers spend most of their mental energy trying to figure out, or decode, the words. With their brains focused on the letters and corresponding sounds, there is little attention left to think about what the words mean. Until readers achieve a basic level of automaticity in word recognition, they are not reading for meaning.

Although most middle school students do have a knowledge of basic phonics, some students fail to develop strategies for using the letter-sound correspondences. They often have difficulty decoding new words, and multisyllabic words are especially problematic. As students encounter longer words they need to be able to break these words into parts.

The lessons on applying multisyllabic rules in Chapter 3 provide students with strategies for tackling longer words. These lessons also provide a basic review of phonics within a model of direct instruction. You can expand this review for students who need more intensive work in this area. You can also skip the basic phonics instruction and focus on multisyllabic word attack strategies.

Using the Most Effective Teaching Strategies

Choosing *how* to teach something is as important as deciding *what* to teach. While a variety of methods are sound, some methods are more effective in teaching specific skills and strategies than others.

Decoding skills need to be taught explicitly and systematically through direct instruction. These skills can be taught to mastery. The lessons in Chapter 3 offer an efficient set of steps and teaching script for short but effective lessons in these skills.

Comprehension skills, however, are developmental skills that are not easily mastered. Students will continue to grow in their understanding of increasingly difficult reading materials throughout life. Comprehension skills can be modeled so that students are shown the thinking processes behind these skills. The lessons in Chapter 2 provide passages and teaching script to model basic comprehension skills.

Establishing a Reading Process

Good readers are strategic in how they approach reading. They consciously or unconsciously do certain things before, during, and after reading. Poor readers, however, often possess few or none of the strategies required for proficient reading. To help struggling readers, establish a routine for reading that involves strategies before, during, and after reading.

- **Before Reading** New ideas presented in reading materials need to be integrated with the reader's **prior knowledge** for understanding to occur. Have students preview the material to see what it is about. Discuss what they already know about the topic and have them **predict** new information they might learn about it. Talk about a **purpose** for reading and have students think about reading strategies they might use with the material.

- **During Reading** Good readers keep track of their understanding as they read. They recognize important or interesting information, know when they don't understand something, and figure out what to do to adjust their understanding. Poor readers are often unaware of these **self-monitoring strategies.** To help these readers become more involved in their reading, suggest that they read with a pencil in hand to jot down notes and questions as they read. If

students own the reading materials, they can mark the text as they read. *The Interactive Readers* that accompany *The Language of Literature* are ideal for this type of work.

- **After Reading** Provide opportunities for readers to reflect on what they have read. These can involve group or class discussion and writing in journals and logs.

Creating a Rich Literary Environment

Students surrounded by books and engaged in thoughtful discussions value the printed word. By incorporating a few basic routines in your classroom schedule, you can provide all students with a rich literary environment.

- **Read aloud.** People of all ages love a good story. Read aloud to your students and hook them on some authors and genres they might not have tackled themselves. For most material, students' listening comprehension is more advanced than their comprehension of written material. Listening helps them develop the thinking skills needed to understand complex text.

- **Write daily.** Encourage students to use writing to work through problems, explore new ideas, or respond to the literature they read. Encourage students to keep journals and learning logs. Writing is a powerful tool to understanding.

- **Read daily.** Allow time for sustained silent reading. Set aside classroom time for students to read self-selected materials. Students who read become better readers, and students are more likely to choose to read if they can pursue ideas they find interesting.

- **Build a classroom library.** If possible, provide a wide range of reading materials so that students are exposed to diverse topics and genres. Respect students' reading choices. Struggling readers first need to view themselves as readers.

- **Promote discussion.** Set ground rules for discussion so that all opinions are heard. Model good discussion behaviors by asking follow-up questions, expanding on ideas presented, and offering alternate ways of viewing topics.

When teachers allocate time to these experiences, students see literacy as valuable.

For people to enjoy reading, they must be able to read fluently; that is, they can read effortlessly and rapidly without running into word identification problems that interfere with comprehension. Readers faced with too many unfamiliar words or complicated sentence structures often put so much effort into figuring out individual words that comprehension eludes them.

How does one become a fluent reader? One way is by reading books and other materials that are a good match for an individual's reading ability. By simply reading materials that are accessible, students' familiarity with written language will grow, along with their confidence in dealing with it. Some educators are so persuaded by the power of accessible reading that they recommend middle school students read a prescribed number of words a year as one way to improve reading skills.

Understanding Reading Levels

Every student reads at a specific level regardless of the grade in which he or she is placed. The reading level will change depending upon the material the student is reading. Reading level in this context is concerned with the relationship between a specific selection or book and a student's ability to read that selection. The following are common terms used to describe these levels:

- **independent level**—The student reads material in which no more than 1 in 20 words is difficult. The material can be read without teacher involvement and is likely to be material students would choose to read on their own.

- **instructional level**—The student reads material in which no more than 2 in 20 words is difficult. The material is most likely found in school and read with teacher involvement.

- **frustration level**—The student reads material in which significantly more than 2 in 20 (or 11 percent) of the words are difficult. Students will probably get little out of reading the material.

It's important to remember that a steady diet of any one reading level isn't a good thing. If students read only material that's too easy, growth in skill and understanding isn't likely. If students read only difficult material, they may give up in frustration much too early.

Using a Student-Directed Informal Reading Inventory

Use the suggestions below to help students find materials that will build fluency.

1. Identify two or more passages consisting of 20 or more words in a selection or book. Have the student read the material silently and then orally. As the student reads aloud, circle words with which he or she has difficulty. Use the following criteria to determine reading level:
   - 1 in 20 difficult words - independent level
   - 2 in 20 difficult words - instructional level
   - More than 2 in 20 words - frustration level

2. To assess the student's choice for independent reading, have the student independently select a book he or she would like to read. The student should open to a random page in the middle of the book (that has not been read before) and begin reading silently from the top of the page. Ask the student to extend one finger on one hand for each time he or she comes across an unfamiliar word. If, by the end of that page, the student has five or more fingers extended, the book is probably too difficult for that student. You may want to suggest the student find a book more suitable to his or her reading level.

Administering a Teacher-Directed Informal Reading Inventory (IRI)

This informal inventory can give an initial idea of a student's reading level. Teachers often use an Informal Reading Inventory (IRI) to place students in the appropriate textbook. You can also use an IRI to help a student find the right books or articles for independent reading.

To conduct an IRI, you need at least one 100-word passage from the material in question, and 10 comprehension questions about the material. If you want more than one passage, select them randomly from every 30th page or so. Have the student read the same passage twice, the first time orally to asses oral reading skills. The student should read the passage a second time silently, after which he or she answers questions for assessment of reading comprehension.

Suggestions for Administering an IRI

1. Tell the student he or she will read the passage aloud, and then again silently. Then tell the student you will ask some questions.

2. Give the student a copy of the passage and keep one for yourself. Have the student read the passage. As the student reads aloud, note on your copy the number of errors he or she makes.

   Mispronunciations: Words that are mispronounced, with the exception of proper nouns.
   Omissions: Words left out that are crucial to understanding a sentence or a concept.
   Additions: Words inserted in a sentence that change the meaning of the text.
   Substitutions: Words substituted for actual words in the text that change the meaning of a sentence. (An acceptable substitution might be the word *hard* for *difficult*.)

   Use these criteria for assessing reading levels after oral reading:
   • Fewer than 3 errors—The student is unlikely to have difficulty decoding text.
   • Between 4 and 9 errors—the student is likely to have difficulty, may need special attention.
   • More than 10 errors—The student is likely to have great difficulty, may need placement in a less demanding reading program.

3. Have the student read the passage again, silently.

4. When the student finishes, ask the comprehension questions you have prepared ahead of time. Tell the student that he or she can look back at the passage before answering a question.

5. Note the number of correct responses. Use these criteria for assessing reading level after silent reading.
   • Eight or more—The student should be able to interpret the selections effectively.
   • Five to seven—The student is likely to have difficulty.
   • Fewer than five—The student needs individual help or alternate placement.

6. Evaluate results from oral and silent reading to decide how good a match the material is for a student's independent or instructional level.

Example Selection

Mother usually said she was too busy to answer my questions. It was a fact that she was overworked, for Grandmother was too old to help her with the heavy work, and she had to try to do both her own work and Father's on our small farm. The rice had to be grown from seeds, and the seedlings transplanted to the paddies, and the paddies tended and harvested. Besides this, she always had to keep one eye on our very active pig to keep him from rooting in our small vegetable patch. She also had to watch our three chickens, who loved to wander away from our farm.

from Dragonwings
by Laurence Yep

Example Comprehension Questions

Answers may vary somewhat but should be similar to those shown in parentheses.

1. What was the narrator's mother usually too busy to do? *(answer questions)*

2. Why was the mother overworked? *(Grandmother was too old to help; Mother did Father's work in addition to her own.)*

3. Where did the mother work? *(on their small farm)*

4. What was grown on their farm? *(rice)*

5. After rice sprouted from seeds, what was done with the seedlings? *(the seedlings were transplanted to the paddies)*

6. What happened after the paddies were taken care of (tended)? *(the paddies were then harvested)*

7. What animal did the mother have to keep her eye on? *(the pig)*

8. Why did the mother have to keep an eye on the pig? *(to keep him from rooting in the vegetable patch)*

9. In addition to the pig, what else did the mother have to watch, and why? *(the three chickens, because they wandered from the farm)*

10. Who do you think is narrating this story? *(either the daughter or the son of the people who own the farm)*

Administering a Cloze Test

Another test that has proven successful in determining reading skill levels is the cloze test. *Cloze* is a psychological term that refers to the human tendency to "bring to closure" a familiar but incomplete pattern. The test is based on "filling in" blanks created in a passage of text unfamiliar to students. The cloze procedure is often used to place students in informational texts, but can also be used in other situations where you want to match a student's reading level with materials.

1. Select a passage of 250 to 300 words that contains a complete thought unit or several paragraphs, preferably from the beginning of the article or book.

2. Delete every fifth word in the passage, excluding the opening sentences.

3. Leave a blank for each word deleted. You should have approximately 50 blanks.

4. For each blank, have students generate the exact word that has been deleted.

5. Use the following to determine reading level:

   • Independent level—58% correct answers or more, or 29 of 50

   • Instructional level—44–57% correct answers, or 22–28 of 50

   • Frustration level—43% correct answers or less or fewer than 21 of 50

Some researchers have modified the cloze procedure as developed by John Bormuth. For example, some have suggested replacing significant words or every tenth word, and accepting synonyms; however, the scoring system above applies only when the process described above is used.

Example Cloze Test

And now he had his boat. Taking the oar, he _____ it against the muddy _____ and pushed with all _____ might. He leaned on _____ oar, and slowly, heavily _____ raft moved into the _____ . It struck on the _____ bottom, and Dewey pushed _____ . He could feel his _____ pounding with the effort. _____ there was a certain _____ , an ease in the _____ . He was afloat! For _____ first time he was _____ . He prepared to sweep _____ oar through the water. _____ had practiced many times _____ shore and he anticipated _____ powerful surge of the _____ .

And then, abruptly, he _____ . His hands clutched the _____ to his chest. He _____ not move at all. _____ did not even breathe. _____ ahead of him, just _____ the river, he had _____ the snort of a _____ .

His father had taken _____ horses to Hunter City _____ pull the wagon, and _____ were no horses here _____ . A pony, he thought— _____ Indian. He waited. He _____ no noise. The raft _____ back against the bank _____ stopped. Still Dewey did _____ move.

The dog at _____ side sensed his caution, _____ he, too, was absolutely _____ . His ears, which usually _____ over his eyes like _____ , were now drawn back.

_____ , silently, Dewey straightened. He _____ toward the cabin. His _____ searched the clearing, the _____ beyond. Nothing. Still his _____ repeated over and over _____ , a pony—an Indian.

from Trouble River
by Betsy Byars

Answers for Cloze Test:

And now he had his boat. Taking the oar, he <u>jammed</u> it against the muddy <u>bank</u> and pushed with all <u>his</u> might. He leaned on <u>the</u> oar, and slowly, heavily <u>the</u> raft moved into the <u>water</u>. It struck on the <u>muddy</u> bottom, and Dewey pushed <u>again</u>. He could feel his <u>head</u> pounding with the effort. <u>Then</u> there was a certain <u>lightness</u>, an ease in the <u>movement</u>. He was afloat! For <u>the</u> first time he was <u>afloat</u>. He prepared to sweep <u>the</u> oar through the water. <u>He</u> had practiced many times <u>on</u> shore and he anticipated <u>the</u> powerful surge of the <u>raft</u>.

Answers for Cloze Test (cont.)

And then, abruptly, he <u>froze</u>. His hands clutched the <u>oar</u> to his chest. He <u>did</u> not move at all. <u>He</u> did not even breathe. <u>For</u> ahead of him, just <u>up</u> the river, he had <u>heard</u> the snort of a <u>pony</u>.

His father had taken <u>both</u> horses to Hunter City <u>to</u> pull the wagon, and <u>there</u> were no horses here <u>now</u>. A pony, he thought—<u>an</u> Indian. He waited. He <u>made</u> no noise. The raft <u>slipped</u> back against the bank <u>and</u> stopped. Still Dewey <u>did</u> <u>not</u> move.

The dog at <u>his</u> side sensed his caution, <u>and</u> he, too, was absolutely <u>still</u>. His ears, which usually <u>flopped</u> over his eyes like <u>eyeshades</u>, were now drawn back.

<u>Carefully</u>, silently, Dewey straightened. He <u>looked</u> toward the cabin. His <u>eyes</u> searched the clearing, the <u>grass</u> beyond. Nothing. Still his <u>mind</u> repeated over and over <u>again</u>, a pony—an Indian.

from Trouble River
by Betsy Byars

Using Degrees of Reading Power (DRP)

Degrees of Reading Power (or DRP) are standardized tests used to measure reading comprehension using the cloze procedure. Results from the tests can be used to measure student progress as well as provide a text difficulty score that forecasts the most difficult material a student can understand at various levels of comprehension. You can use this information to match a student's DRP score with individual books. See *Suggested Literature from the Literature Connections* on page 7.

Using Repeated Oral Reading to Improve Fluency

Repeated oral reading of passages is an effective technique for improving fluency. Beginning readers have trouble with fluency because they often focus on decoding rather than comprehension. However, more advanced readers will decode text automatically, thus deriving more meaning from what they read.

Word recognition skills increase through three stages:

- Nonaccurate stage—great difficulty with word recognition, even when adequate time is provided

- Accuracy stage—printed words are recognizable with focused attention

- Automatic stage—comprehension of unfamiliar material achieved through oral reading; student reads quickly and with inflection

Selected passages might be brief, thought-provoking excerpts from literature, and should be chosen with students' interests and current ability level in mind. For this exercise, you may choose to pair students of differing reading abilities together, or use this as a one-on-one teacher-student activity.

1. Select an excerpt within the student's reading level that ranges from 50 to 200 words in length.

2. Student reads the passage out loud to a partner. The partner records the number of reading errors, noting how many seconds the student takes to read the passage.

3. Read the passage out loud for the class so students can hear it read correctly.

4. As homework or an in-class assignment, students practice reading the passage out loud on their own.

5. After practice, students read the passage aloud again while a partner records the speed and the number of recognition errors.

6. After repeated practice and readings, the student will begin to read the passage fluently and achieve an acceptable level of accuracy. Note that the speed is the critical factor rather than 100% accuracy.

<u>Example Selection:</u>

I have a little dream

For the flying of a plane.
I have a little scheme,
I'll follow yet again.

There is a little heaven,
Just around the hill.
I haven't seen it for a long time,
But I know it's waiting still.

from Dragonwings
by Laurence Yep

Suggested Literature from the Literature Connections

BOOK	average estimated Dale-Chall grade	average estimated DRP score	DRP booklink
The Cay	6.4	55.2	54
Dogsong	5.9	53.9	51
Dragonwings	5.9	53.3	54
The House of Dies Drear	5.6	52.3	49
Island of the Blue Dolphins	6.2	55.3	52
Maniac Magee	6.2	55.3	52
Number the Stars	6.2	55.8	52
Trouble River	5.9	53.5	51
Tuck Everlasting	7.2	58.8	56
A Wrinkle in Time	5.9	53.5	51
Call of the Wild	9.0	61.2	62
The Clay Marble	5.5	51.6	48
Homecoming	5.5	51.6	48
I, Juan de Pareja	7.8	60.9	58
Roll of Thunder, Hear My Cry	8.0	61.8	53
The True Confessions of Charlotte Doyle	7.5	54.7	52
Where the Red Fern Grows	5.5	49.3	47
The Witch of Blackbird Pond	7.0	58.0	57
Across Five Aprils	6.9	57.1	59
The Contender	5.7	54.0	50
The Giver	7.2	59.6	56
The Glory Field	5.9	53.5	51
In My Father's House	6.8	56.6	55
Johnny Tremain	6.8	56.6	55
Nothing But the Truth	5.5	49.4	47
So Far from the Bamboo Grove	5.3	51.8	50
Taking Sides	6.5	55.5	52

The Language of Literature provides an extensive instructional plan for grades 6 through 8, including systematic and direct instruction in the pupil's edition as well as comprehensive lessons in the teacher's edition. The instruction in *The Language of Literature* will enable the majority of students to master the skills taught with each selection; however, from time to time you may need to enhance your teaching for students who need more direct instruction in specific skills. For these students, explicit instruction and reciprocal teaching prove highly effective.

Explicit Instruction

Explicit instruction is a three-part process for teaching strategies and definitions. First, demonstrate for your students the skill you are teaching. Second, have students practice and apply the skill you just demonstrated. To conclude, offer feedback to students about their application of the skill.

An effective way to use explicit instruction in the classroom is to model the skill. When you model, you demonstrate a way of resolving questions about unfamiliar material by "thinking through" questions out loud, thereby modeling a thought process for the students. Here is an example of how a you might model the skill of inferencing by using the paragraph below.

Example Selection

(from "Zebra" by Chaim Potok)

Then, a year ago, racing down Franklin Avenue, he had given himself that push and had begun to turn into an eagle, when a huge rushing shadow appeared in his line of vision, and crashed into him and plunged him into a darkness from which he emerged very, very slowly. . .

Example Modeling

I'm not sure what happened to the boy, but I can make inferences by looking for clues in the sentences. When I make an inference, I make a logical guess about something based on the text and my own knowledge or experience. This paragraph says that the boy had "begun to turn into an eagle". Because I read earlier that he is a fast runner, this must mean that he ran so fast it seemed he was flying like an eagle. A "huge rushing shadow" must mean something big, like a truck, was moving quickly. The phrase "appeared in his line of vision" probably means that he wasn't expecting to see it. The shadow "crashed into him and plunged him into a darkness". This could mean he had an accident with a big truck, and it is taking him a long time to recover.

As the example shows, by modeling your thought process for students you provide a clear example of how they can learn and apply the skills they find most challenging. After you have modeled this for them, give each student a chance to try it on his or her own. Offer feedback based on the skill he or she demonstrated.

The pages in the next section provide mini-lessons with opportunities to practice modeling the most frequently taught comprehension skills.

Reciprocal Teaching

Reciprocal teaching is a technique in which the burden of asking comprehension questions gradually moves from you onto your students. To use this technique, first teach students four basic reciprocal teaching strategies. These strategies comprise the "game plan" for reading:

- **Question gathering**—Students identify important information in the content, form questions about content, and address their questions to peers.

- **Summarizing**—Students summarize the most important information in a specific passage.

- **Clarifying**—Students identify problems the passage presents, such as difficulty with vocabulary or comprehension.

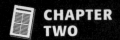

- **Predicting**—Students rely on prior knowledge and information already presented to predict what the author will discuss in subsequent paragraphs.

Once the strategies have been introduced, model for your students the way in which good readers employ each strategy by leading the entire dialogue. After reading the next expository passage, appoint a student to share in the question-asking.

Below is an example selection followed by an example dialogue in which Student 1 has been selected to share some of the burden of asking comprehension questions, while the teacher continues to guide the dialogue.

Example Selection

More than 35,000 cowboys rode herd along the Texas cattle trails. Although folklore and picture postcards depicted the cowboy as Anglo-American, about 25 percent were African American and another 12 percent were Mexican vaqueros—cowboys who had worked in Texas since the days before Texas's independence. There were Native American cowboys, too, and a few women.

Example Dialogue

Teacher: What questions do you have for the class?

Student 1: My question is: Were all cowboys Anglo-American?

Student 2: No, 25 percent were African American.

Student 1: What about the rest?

Student 3: Twelve percent were Mexican.

Student 4: Some were Native American and women.

Student 2: The rest were Anglo-Americans.

Teacher: What is your summary of this passage?

Student 1: My summary is: From the stories and pictures we see, many people think all cowboys were Anglo-American, but almost 40 percent were minorities.

Teacher: Does anything need to be clarified?

Student 1: We should clarify *vaqueros*.

Teacher: Is *vaqueros* defined here?

Student 5: Yes, *vaqueros* were Mexican cowboys who worked in Texas before it was independent.

Teacher: What do you predict the next paragraph will be about?

Student 6: I think the author will talk about Native Americans and women as cowboys.

Student 7: The author might also tell us more about the *vaqueros*.

As students become increasingly familiar with participating in reciprocal teaching, they will take on more responsibility for leading the dialogue. You should continue to guide the discussion, keeping students mindful of using the four strategies as a framework for their discussion.

1 For students who have trouble grasping the main idea of a paragraph or passage, discuss these points.

- The main idea is the most important idea that a writer tries to make in a paragraph or passage.

- The writer may state the main idea in a sentence. This sentence can appear at the beginning, middle, or end of a paragraph or passage.

- The writer may not always state the main idea. Sometimes it is implied. The reader must then figure it out by thinking about the details and putting the main idea in his or her own words.

2 Duplicate the following paragraph. A copymaster is provided on page 13. Have students follow along as you read it aloud, using it to model the **stated main idea**.

> Some of the world's best-known games were invented centuries ago. For example, historians believe that checkers was first played in Egypt almost 3,600 years ago. Recent discoveries show that chess was invented at least 1,400 years ago.

You could say: Writers often put the main idea in the first sentence so that readers will know what to expect in the rest of the paragraph. "Some of the world's best-known games were invented centuries ago" seems like the main idea. The second sentence tells me that checkers was first played almost 4,000 years ago. It also contains the phrase "for example" that signals a detail rather than a main idea.

The third sentence says that chess was invented more than fourteen centuries ago. Both sentences are details that support the first sentence. Therefore the first sentence does state the main idea.

3 Duplicate the following paragraph. A copymaster is provided on page 13. Have students follow along as you read it aloud, using it to model the **implied main idea**.

> Chess started in India about 500 A.D. It was called *chaturanga* and was based on an Indian army formation. The Persians were the next people to play the game. Their word for the king chess piece was *shah*. The English word *chess* originated from *shah*.

You could say: I'll look again in the first sentence for the main idea. It tells me when chess started. However, the second sentence also tells me another detail about chess. In fact, each sentence gives another detail about chess. In this case the writer chose not to state the main idea. I'll have to figure it out. All of the sentences either tell about how chess started or the origin of its name. Therefore, the main idea is a brief history of chess.

4 Duplicate the following paragraphs and read them aloud. A copymaster is provided on page 14.

> Lacrosse was a popular pastime in North America long before the arrival of European explorers. Unlike modern baseball, which is thought of as an "American" sport but actually originated elsewhere, lacrosse was developed in North America without outside influence. Forms of this game appear to have originated among several Native American groups.
>
> Lacrosse was a brutal sport with games lasting for several days. Some thought the games were a good way to prepare for battle. Lacrosse was also a part of native religious beliefs and appeared in native myths and legends.

5 Duplicate and distribute the Main Idea Web on the next page. Have students work in pairs to fill in the webs with main ideas and details from both paragraphs. Correct responses are shown in the Answer Key on page 33.

6 Make additional copies of the Main Idea Web and have them available for students to use with the following selections from *The Language of Literature*.

Grade 6
from *All I Really Need to Know I Learned in Kindergarten* by Robert Fulghum
"Matthew Henson at the Top of the World" by Jim Haskins

Grade 7
from *Immigrant Kids* by Russell Freedman
from *Long Walk to Freedom* by Nelson Mandela

Grade 8
"The Great Rat Hunt" by Laurence Yep
from *Grand Mothers* by Nikki Giovanni

Name _____ Date _____

Main Idea	Details

Name _____ Date _____

Some of the world's best-known games were invented centuries ago. For example, historians believe that checkers was first played in Egypt almost 3,600 years ago. Recent discoveries show that chess was invented at least 1,400 years ago.

Chess started in India about 500 A.D. It was called *chaturanga* and was based on an Indian army formation. The Persians were the next people to play the game. Their word for the king chess piece was *shah*. The English word *chess* originated from *shah*.

Name _____ Date _____

Lacrosse was a popular pastime in North America long before the arrival of European explorers. Unlike modern baseball, which is thought of as an "American" sport but actually originated elsewhere, lacrosse was developed in North America without outside influence. Forms of this game appear to have originated among several Native American groups.

Lacrosse was a brutal sport with games lasting for several days. Some thought the games were a good way to prepare for battle. Lacrosse was also a part of native religious beliefs and appeared in native myths and legends.

1 Ask students if they have ever told a friend a story with events that weren't in the exact order in which they happened. If details were out of order, the friend could ask questions to clarify the sequence. Explain that it is important to keep track of the sequence of events in order to understand the meaning a of story or how the plot moves forward, especially since the writer isn't available to answer questions. The following points will be useful to students who need more help.

- Sequence is the order in which events happen. Sequence refers to the chronological order in a story or a piece of nonfiction. It may also refer to steps in a process or in following directions.

- Writers sometimes use words such as *first, next, after, before, then,* and *later* to connect ideas and indicate the order in which events occur.

- Words, phrases, or dates that tell when something is happening can also help readers figure out the sequence of events.

- The order of the events may not be the same as the order of the sentences in a paragraph or story. A paragraph or story may begin telling about an event that happens in the present. Other sentences may tell about events that happened in the past leading up to the present.

- When events are not clearly laid out, it may help the reader to visualize in his or her mind how the events happened.

2 Duplicate the following paragraph. A copymaster is provided on page 17. Have students to follow along as you read it aloud, using it to model **sequence**.

> Emanuel topped off a perfect day by eating fried chicken for dinner. That morning, he and his family had decided to make the day a vacation day. They had loaded up the car and headed into the city for a visit to the natural history museum. The trip turned out better than they had imagined. There was so much to see at the museum that they didn't return home until sunset.

You could say: The first sentence tells me Emanuel ended a perfect day by making dinner. This sentence is a clue to events that may have happened earlier in the day. Chances are that the first sentence is not the first event in the paragraph. The second and third sentences tells me that Emanuel's family went to a museum in the morning. The last two sentences tell about the museum visit and the trip home. So the visit to the museum happened first, the trip home was next, and dinner was last.

3 Duplicate the following paragraph. A copymaster is provided on page 17. Have students follow along as you read it aloud.

> As Emanuel and his family drove home, he thought about their visit to the museum. Upon their arrival that morning, they went to see the new exhibit about bats. Next, he took his parents to see the prehistoric animal skeletons. At noon, they walked to the cafeteria for lunch. After they finished, they went to see the show at the planetarium. By the time the show was over, it was almost 5 P.M. There was just enough time to hurry back to the bat exhibit for one last look.

4 Duplicate and distribute the Sequence/Flow Chart on the next page. Work with students to fill in the first event. Then have them complete the chart. Tell students to highlight any words or phrases that helped them determine the order of events. Ask volunteers to share how they mapped out the events of the paragraph. Possible responses are shown in the Answer Key on page 33.

5 Make additional copies of the chart on page 16 and have it available for students to use with the following selections from *The Language of Literature.*

Grade 6
"President Cleveland, Where Are You?" by Robert Cormier
"Summer of Fire" by Patricia Lauber
"Abd al-Rahman Ibrahima" by Walter Dean Myers

Grade 7
"Eleanor Roosevelt" by William Jay Jacobs

Grade 8
"The Story of an Eyewitness" by Jack London
"The Bet" by Anton Chekhov

Sequence/Flow Chart

Name _____ Date _____

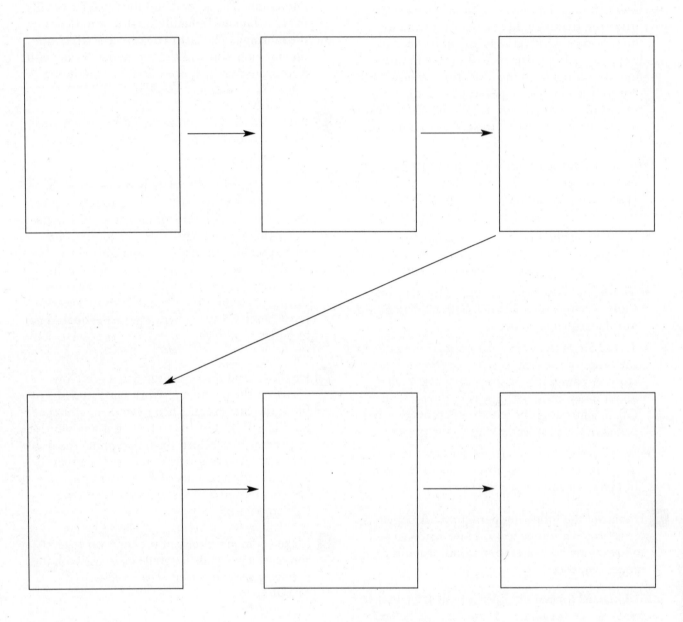

Name _____ Date _____

Emanuel topped off a perfect day by eating fried chicken for dinner. That morning, he and his family had decided to make the day a vacation day. They had loaded up the car and headed into the city for a visit to the natural history museum. The trip turned out better than they had imagined. There was so much to see at the museum that they didn't return home until sunset.

As Emanuel and his family drove home, he thought about their visit to the museum. Upon their arrival that morning, they went to see the new exhibit about bats. Next, he took his parents to see the prehistoric animal skeletons. At noon, they walked to the cafeteria for lunch. After they finished, they went to see the show at the planetarium. By the time the show was over, it was almost 5 P.M. There was just enough time to hurry back to the bat exhibit for one last look.

1 Write the following sentence on the board, and read it aloud.

> We will have physical education inside today because it is raining.

Ask students which event caused the other event to happen. *(The rain caused us to have physical education inside.)* Introduce cause and effect by discussing the following points.

- A **cause** is an action or event that makes something else happen.

- An **effect** is what happens because of a certain action or event.

Explain cause-and-effect relationships may contain one or more or these characteristics.

- Writers use clue words or phrases *(because, since, as a result)* to indicate causes and effects. However, clue words alone do not automatically indicate a cause-and-effect relationship. One event must make another event happen.

- A single cause can result in more than one effect. Also, several causes can lead to a single effect. *(The rain caused us to have physical education inside and miss our afternoon field trip to the outdoor theater.* or *Because it was cloudy and the bus had a faulty brake, we cancelled our outdoor field trip.)*

- Sometimes a series of events are linked in a cause-and-effect chain in which one event causes another, which in turn causes another, and so on. *(Because it snowed, Ray couldn't leave the house. Because he couldn't leave the house to buy food, he ran out of milk and bread.)*

Watch out for events that happen in sequence. Just because one event follows another doesn't mean the first event caused the second one. *After it rained, we found the shoe.* (We didn't find the shoe because it stopped raining.)

2 Duplicate the following paragraph or use the copymaster on page 20. Ask students to follow along as you read it aloud, using it to model **cause-and-effect.**

> Michael stayed home because he had the flu. He slept most of the day. Since he had to stay home, he missed the math quiz. After he returned to school, he studied for the quiz.

You could say: The first sentence has a clue word that may indicate a cause-and-effect relationship. Having the flu caused Michael to stay home. It's logical that the flu would cause other effects. The next sentence doesn't contain any clue words, but it's reasonable that the flu would make him so tired he would sleep all day. In the next sentence the clue word *since* tells me that staying home caused him to miss the math quiz.

The first and third sentences are linked in a cause-and-effect chain. The flu caused Michael to stay home, which caused him to miss the quiz. The last sentence is not part of a cause-and-effect relationship but shows a sequence of events.

3 Write on the board these signal words: *because, so, since, as a result.* Duplicate the following paragraph or use the copymaster on page 20. Have students follow as you read it aloud.

> When Johanna and Gabriel finally reached the top of the mountain, they sat down to rest. "Whew, I'm thirsty," said Johanna. Gabriel pulled a water bottle out of his backpack and handed it to her. When Johanna tried to drink, however, all the water spilled because the lid was not screwed tightly. As a result, they were forced to ask other hikers if they had brought extra water.

4 Duplicate and distribute the Cause-and-Effect Chart on the next page. Work with students to fill in the first cause-and-effect relationship. Possible responses are shown in the Answer Key on page 33.

5 Make copies of the chart on page 19 and have it available for students to use with these and other selections from *The Language of Literature.*

Grade 6
"Nadia the Willful" by Sue Alexander
"Lob's Girl" by Joan Aiken

Grade 7
"Thank You, M'am" by Langston Hughes
"The War of the Wall" by Toni Cade Bambara

Grade 8
"Raymond's Run" by Toni Cade Bambara
The Million-Pound Bank Note by Mark Twain, dramatized by Walter Hackett

Cause-and-Effect Chart

Name _____ Date _____

Cause(s)	→	Effect(s)

Name _____ Date _____

Michael stayed home because he had the flu. He slept most of the day. Since he had to stay home, he missed the math quiz. After he returned to school, he studied for the quiz.

When Johanna and Gabriel finally reached the top of the mountain, they sat down to rest.

"Whew, I'm thirsty," said Johanna. Gabriel pulled a water bottle out of his backpack and handed it to her. When Johanna tried to drink, however, all the water spilled because the lid was not screwed tightly. As a result, they were forced to ask other hikers if they had brought extra water.

1 The following points will be helpful to students who have trouble understanding the terms compare and contrast.

- **Comparing** means to think about the ways in the which two or more people or two or more things are alike. *(The dress and the jacket are red.)* Writers sometimes use words such as *both, same, alike, like, also, similarly,* and *too* to make comparisons. *(The dress and the jacket are* <u>both</u> *red.)*

- **Contrasting** means to think about ways in which two or more people or two or more things are different. *(Jillian's favorite food is pizza. Lorenzo's favorite food is French fries.)* Writers sometimes use words or phrases such as *unlike, but, although, instead, yet, even though, however,* and *on the other hand* to contrast two or more things. *(Jillian's favorite food is pizza,* <u>unlike</u> *Lorenzo, whose favorite food is French fries.)*

- Sometimes there are no signal words. Readers must figure out what the writer is comparing and contrasting from the details given.

2 Duplicate the following paragraph. A copymaster is provided on page 23. Have students follow along as you read it aloud, using it to model **comparison-and-contrast.**

> Nadia and Jason are both die-hard swimmers. Nadia loves to swim in the ocean or in a small lake where she vacations with her family. She rarely swims at a pool because it's usually too crowded. On the other hand, Jason is frightened by the giant waves of the ocean and prefers to swim in a pool.

You could say: The first sentence tells me that two people—Nadia and Jason—are being compared. The first sentence also contains the word *both,* which signals a way in which Nadia and Jason are alike. The second sentence gives me more information about Nadia. The fact that the sentence is only about Nadia is a clue that the information presented about her may be different from information later presented about Jason. My hunch proves to be right.

The last sentence begins with the phrase *On the other hand,* which signals a difference

between Nadia and Jason. Therefore, Nadia and Jason are alike in that they both swim. The difference is that Jason will only swim in a pool and Nadia will swim anywhere.

3 For reference, write on the board the signal words and phrases listed in the second bulleted item. Then duplicate the following paragraph and read it aloud. A copymaster is provided on page 23.

> Cherries and apples are two of the most popular fruits in this country. Both are known for their refreshing juiciness and rich color, and both make delicious pies. However, their similarities stop there. Cherries, being small, grow in clusters and are available only in the summer. Apples, on the other hand, are medium-sized fruits that grow individually and are available year-round.

4 Duplicate and distribute the Venn Diagram on the next page. Have students fill in the diagram, using information in the paragraph along with what they already know about cherries and apples to compare and contrast the two fruits.

5 Have volunteers share the information in their diagrams by first describing the similarities between the two types of fruits and then describing the differences. Possible responses are shown in the Answer Key on page 34.

6 Make additional copies of the diagram on page 22 and have it available for students to use with the following selections from *The Language of Literature.*

Grade 6
"The Sand Castle" by Alma Luz Villanueva

Grade 7
"A Retrieved Reformation" by O. Henry

Grade 8
"I Stepped from Plank to Plank" by Emily Dickinson
"Child on Top of a Greenhouse" by Theodore Roethke

Name _____ Date _____

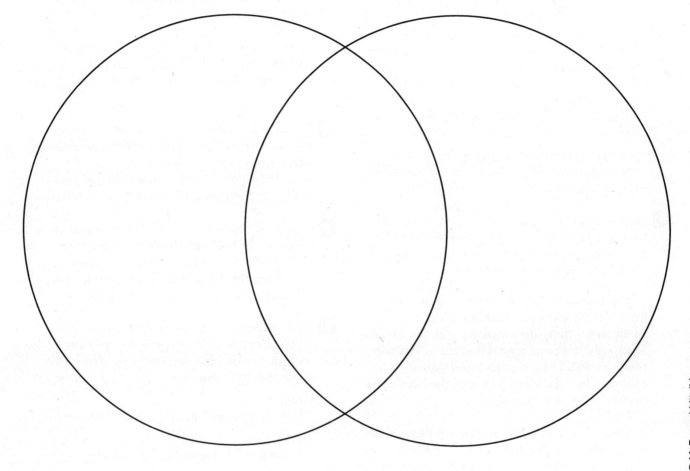

Name _____ Date _____

Nadia and Jason are both die-hard swimmers. Nadia loves to swim in the ocean or in a small lake where she vacations with her family. She rarely swims at a pool because it's usually too crowded. On the other hand, Jason is frightened by the giant waves of the ocean and prefers to swim in a pool.

Cherries and apples are two of the most popular fruits in this country. Both are known for their refreshing juiciness and rich color, and both make delicious pies. However, their similarities stop there. Cherries, being small, grow in clusters and are available only in the summer. Apples, on the other hand, are medium-sized fruits that grow individually and are available year-round.

1 Present students with the following situation: *The door is open and the light is on when you arrive for class. One day the door is closed and the light is off. What inference can you make?* (Students will most likely say that the teacher is absent or late for class.) For students who need more help making inferences, discuss the following points:

- It is not possible for writers to include every detail about what is happening in a work of literature.

- Often writers purposely choose to hint at details rather than state them; this can add meaning and suspense for the reader.

- Inferences are logical guesses based on clues in the text and on the reader's own knowledge and common sense.

- To make inferences, readers must: look for details that the writer provides about character, setting, and events; think about what they already know about a topic; and connect the story to their own personal experiences.

2 Duplicate the following paragraph. A copymaster is provided on page 26. Ask students to follow along as you read it aloud, using it to model the skill **making inferences**.

> The sun was just rising, but Tonya already had her swimsuit on underneath her sweats. The wetsuit and surfboard she'd borrowed were beside the front door. She sat on the sofa, staring at the clock and tapping her foot while she waited for her friends to arrive.

You could say: The first sentence tells me that Tonya was up rather early to prepare to go swimming. The second sentence tells me that she had all her equipment ready at the front door. Since she borrowed the equipment, she probably doesn't surf very often. So she's very excited about going. In the last sentence, Tonya is staring at the clock and tapping her foot. People often stare at the clock when they are concerned if someone is going to be on time. Tapping the foot is a nervous habit. So Tonya is probably impatient and possibly worried that her friends may not arrive on time.

3 Duplicate the following passage. A copymaster is provided on page 26. Have students to follow along as you read it aloud.

> Sam and his father pulled up in their red minivan at 6 o'clock sharp. Trish was in the middle seat, and the gear was stowed in the back. Tonya wrote a note to her parents telling them that she'd be back from surf camp in time to take her dog Rip for a walk. Then she carried her board and wetsuit to the van. As Tonya settled into her seat, Sam told her that the waves were supposed to be huge.
>
> "Great!" exclaimed Tonya. However, before the van had pulled away from the curb, she was busily biting her nails.

4 Duplicate and distribute the Inference/Judgment Chart on the next page. Work with students to fill in the first row. Then have them add to the chart any other inferences they make about the passage. Sample responses are shown in the Answer Key on page 34.

5 Make additional copies of the chart on page 25 and have it available for students to use with the following selections from *The Language of Literature*.

Grade 6
"A Life in the Day of Gary Paulsen"
"I'm Nobody! Who Are You?" by Emily Dickinson
"It Seems I Test People" by James Berry
"Growing Pains" by Jean Little
"The Circuit" by Francisco Jiménez

Grade 7
"Zebra" by Chaim Potok
"One Ordinary Day, with Peanuts" by Shirley Jackson
"An Hour with Abuelo" by Judith Ortiz Cofer

Grade 8
"Flowers for Algernon" by Daniel Keyes
"Rules of the Game" by Amy Tan
"A Journey" by Nikki Giovanni
"Knoxville, Tennessee" by Nikki Giovanni
"Rain, Rain, Go Away" by Isaac Asimov
from *Roughing It* by Mark Twain

Inference/Judgment Chart

Name _____ Date _____

Selection Information	+	My Opinion/ What I Know	=	My Inference/ My Judgment
	+		=	
	+		=	
	+		=	
	+		=	

Name _____ Date _____

The sun was just rising, but Tonya already had her swimsuit on underneath her sweats. The wetsuit and surfboard she'd borrowed were beside the front door. She sat on the sofa, staring at the clock and tapping her foot while she waited for her friends to arrive.

Sam and his father pulled up in their red minivan at 6 o'clock sharp. Trish was in the middle seat, and the gear was stowed in the back. Tonya wrote a note to her parents telling them that she'd be back from surf camp in time to take her dog Rip for a walk. Then she carried her board and wetsuit to the van. As Tonya settled into her seat, Sam told her that the waves were supposed to be huge.

"Great!" exclaimed Tonya. However, before the van had pulled away from the curb, she was busily biting her nails.

1 To introduce the concept of predicting, ask students to make a guess about what the weather will be like in a few hours based on what they already know. Use the following points to explain how the strategy applies to reading a story.

- When you **predict,** you try to figure out what will happen next based upon what has already happened.

- To make a **prediction,** you must combine clues in a story plus your own knowledge and experience to make a reasonable guess.

- Good readers make and revise predictions about characters, setting, and plot as they read. Sometimes they don't even realize they're doing it.

- Sometimes you must first make a guess or inference about what is happening before you can predict what will happen next. *(Pedro felt the cold wind through his light jacket. I can't wait for this bus much longer.)* You might infer that Pedro didn't realize it was so cold when he walked to the bus stop. You could then use the inference to predict that he will return home to put on warmer clothes.

2 Duplicate the following paragraph. A copymaster is provided on page 29. Have students follow along as you read it aloud, using it to model the skill of **predicting.**

> Sarah held her jaw as she slowly trudged down the stairs and seated herself in the kitchen for breakfast.

You could say: **The first sentence tells me that Sarah is holding her jaw. A person sometimes holds his or her jaw when he or she has a toothache. I'll read further to see if my prediction is right.**

> "Is that bacon? she asked as she grabbed a strip and made half of it disappear.

You could say: **The second sentence tells me that Sarah just ate some bacon. Since I think she has a toothache, the bacon may make her feel worse. I'll read further to see if I'm on target.**

> "Ow, my tooth is killing me!" Sarah cried out. Her mother reached for the phone.

You could say: **My predictions were right. Based on what had just happened to Sarah, I can also predict that her mother is calling the dentist in the last sentence.**

3 Duplicate the following paragraph. A copymaster is provided on page 29. Instruct students to follow along, as you read it aloud. Afterwards, students should be ready to infer what has happened and to predict what will happen next.

> The sun shone brightly in Pecos on June 17, 2030. Mrs. Toliver wiped her brow and fanned herself with the newspaper she bought at the corner stand. She started to open the paper, but a voice interrupted her.
>
> "Good day, Ma'am," shouted the store clerk. "Mr. Rojas called the Weather Bureau and ordered a really hot day for his pool party. Everyone in town will be there. You're going, aren't you?"
>
> "Oh, no. I made other plans months ago," replied Mrs. Toliver, trying to cover up the fact that she hadn't received an invitation.
>
> "So he didn't invite me," she mumbled to herself when she was well past the store. "Well, he doesn't realize that I have more power with the Weather Bureau than he does."

4 Duplicate and distribute the Predicting chart on the next page. Have students work in pairs to complete the chart. Possible responses are shown in the Answer Key on page 35.

5 Make additional copies of the chart on page 28 and have it available for students to use with the following selections from *The Language of Literature.*

Grade 6
"Ghost of the Lagoon" by Armstrong Perry
"Aaron's Gift" by Myron Levoy
"Cricket in the Road" by Michael Anthony

Grade 7
"Rikki-tikki-tavi" by Rudyard Kipling
"Amigo Brothers" by Piri Thomas
"The White Umbrella" by Gish Jen

Grade 8
"Checkouts" by Cynthia Rylant
"The Ransom of Red Chief" by O. Henry
The Hitchhiker by Lucille Fletcher

Predicting Chart

Name _____ Date _____

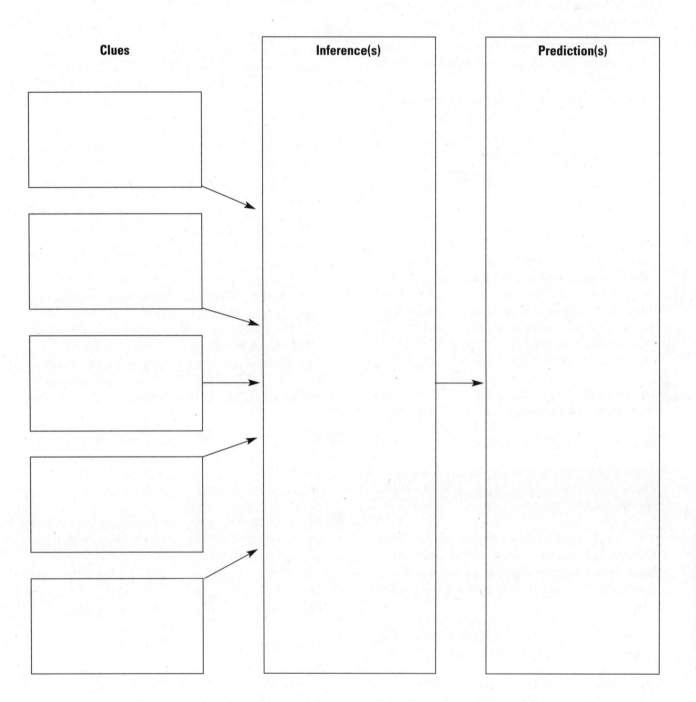

Clues

Inference(s)

Prediction(s)

Name _____ Date _____

Sarah held her jaw as she slowly trudged down the stairs and seated herself in the kitchen for breakfast.

"Is that bacon? she asked as she grabbed a strip and made half of it disappear.

"Ow, my tooth is killing me!" Sarah cried out. Her mother reached for the phone.

The sun shone brightly in Pecos on June 17, 2030. Mrs. Toliver wiped her brow and fanned herself with the newspaper she bought at the corner stand. She started to open the paper, but a voice interrupted her.

"Good day, Ma'am," shouted the store clerk. "Mr. Rojas called the Weather Bureau and ordered a really hot day for his pool party. Everyone in town will be there. You're going, aren't you?"

"Oh, no. I made other plans months ago," replied Mrs. Toliver, trying to cover up the fact that she hadn't received an invitation.

"So he didn't invite me," she mumbled to herself when she was well past the store. "Well, he doesn't realize that I have more power with the Weather Bureau than he does."

1 Use examples from textbooks, newspapers, magazines, etc. as you discuss the following points about distinguishing fact and opinion.

- A **fact** is a statement that can be proven through observation, experience, and research. A fact may include supporting evidence such as statistics or quotations from a recognized expert.

- An **opinion** is a statement that tells what a writer thinks, believes, or feels about a subject. It cannot be proven true or false.

- A writer may use words and phrases such as the following to signal an opinion: *according to, I think, in my opinion, perhaps, seem, ought to, should, bad, good, better, worse, excellent, terrible.* A writer may also use words that appeal to the reader's emotions.

- Sometimes a writer will use one or more facts to support an opinion.

- A single statement can contain both a fact and an opinion.

- A statement that you agree with is not necessarily a fact.

2 Duplicate the following paragraph. A copymaster is provided on page 32. Have students follow along as you read it aloud, using it to model the skill of **distinguishing between fact and opinion.**

> Watching soap operas on television is a waste of time. Although the "soaps" dramatize real life, they aren't nearly as interesting as the real thing. From one week to the next, nothing new ever seems to happen on these shows.

You could say: Actually, I agree with the point the writer is making, but I know these statements may not be facts. First, I look for numbers, statistics, or quotations from experts. If I don't find any, there's a good chance that the statements are the writer's opinion.

Next, I look for words that might signal opinions. The first sentence contains the phrase *waste of time.* This is pretty negative language. The statement also can't be proven. The second sentence is tricky. It states the fact that soaps dramatize real life, but the second part of the sentence states an opinion that can't be proven. The last sentence uses the signal word *seems,*

and also can't be proven.

3 For reference, write on the board the signal words and phrases listed in the third bulleted item. Then duplicate the following paragraph and read it aloud. A copymaster is provided on page 32.

> Real-life crime shows, in my opinion, are the best thing on television. In addition to being entertaining, these shows have helped bring criminals to justice. I think too many criminals get away with their crimes. By giving details about the crimes and showing pictures of suspects, these shows give the public a chance to help catch them. Everyone ought to watch the shows and share any information they may have about the crimes and the suspects.

4 Duplicate and distribute the Two-Column Chart on the next page and ask students to use it to list the facts and opinions in the paragraph. Suggest that they highlight any signal words that helped them distinguish between the two types of statements.

5 Have volunteers share their completed charts, explaining why they listed each statement where they did. Correct responses are shown in the Answer Key on page 35.

6 Make additional copies of the chart on page 31 and have it available for students to use with the following selections from *The Language of Literature.*

Grade 6
"Chinatown" by Laurence Yep
"The Dog of Pompeii" by Louis Untermeyer

Grade 7
from *Exploring the* Titanic by Robert D. Ballard

Grade 8
from *Undaunted Courage* by Stephen E. Ambrose
"Block Party" by Jewell Parker Rhodes

Name _____ Date _____

Fact	Opinion

Name _____ Date _____

Watching soap operas on television is a waste of time. Although the "soaps" dramatize real life, they aren't nearly as interesting as the real thing. From one week to the next, nothing new ever seems to happen on these shows.

Real-life crime shows, in my opinion, are the best thing on television. In addition to being entertaining, these shows have helped bring criminals to justice. I think too many criminals get away with their crimes. By giving details about the crimes and showing pictures of suspects, these shows give the public a chance to help catch them. Everyone ought to watch the shows and share any information they may have about the crimes and the suspects.

Answer Key

Name _____ Date _____

Main Idea and Supporting Details

Main Idea	Details
Paragraph 1: Main Idea: Lacrosse was a popular sport in North America before the arrival of European explorers. Paragraph 2: Main Idea (implied): For certain tribes, lacrosse became an important way of life.	• Lacrosse developed in American without foreign influences. • It was first played by several Native American groups. • Lacrosse was a brutal sport with games lasting several days. • Some thought it was good preparation for battle. • It was part of religious beliefs and appeared in myths and legends.

Sequence Flow Chart

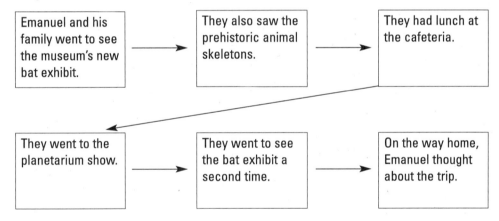

Cause-and-Effect Chart

Causes	→	Effect(s)
Gabriel and Johanna had been climbing.	→	They reached the top of the mountain. They sat down to rest. Johanna became thirsty.
Johanna said she was thirsty.	→	Gabriel gave her a water bottle.
The lid was not screwed tightly.	→	All the water spilled.
Gabriel and Johanna had no water to drink.	→	They had to ask other hikers for extra water.

Name _____ Date _____

Compare and Contrast

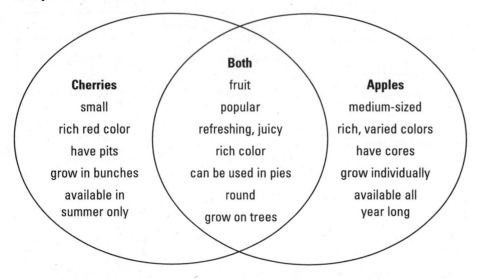

Cherries
small
rich red color
have pits
grow in bunches
available in summer only

Both
fruit
popular
refreshing, juicy
rich color
can be used in pies
round
grow on trees

Apples
medium-sized
rich, varied colors
have cores
grow individually
available all year long

Making Inferences

Selection Information	+	My Opinion/What I Know	=	My judgment/My Inference
Tonya is going to surf camp and will be home in time to walk her dog.	+	People surf in the ocean.	=	Tonya lives near the ocean.
Tonya wrote that she'd be back in time to walk her dog.	+	Pet owners have to consider their pets when they leave home for extended periods.	=	Tonya is a responsible pet owner.
Tonya said "Great!" but started to bite her nails after she heard about the big waves.	+	People sometimes bite their nails when they are nervous.	=	Tonya is nervous about surfing on the big waves.

Name _____ Date _____

Predicting

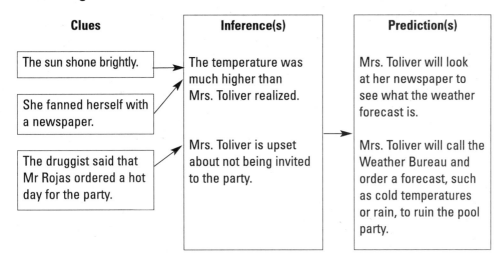

Clues

| The sun shone brightly. |
| She fanned herself with a newspaper. |
| The druggist said that Mr Rojas ordered a hot day for the party. |

Inference(s)

The temperature was much higher than Mrs. Toliver realized.

Mrs. Toliver is upset about not being invited to the party.

Prediction(s)

Mrs. Toliver will look at her newspaper to see what the weather forecast is.

Mrs. Toliver will call the Weather Bureau and order a forecast, such as cold temperatures or rain, to ruin the pool party.

Fact and Opinion

Fact	Opinion
• These shows have helped bring criminals to justice. • By giving details about the crimes and showing pictures of the suspects, these shows give the public a chance to help catch them.	• Real-life crime shows, in my opinion, are the best thing on television. • These shows are also entertaining. • I think too many criminals get away with their crimes. • Everyone ought to watch the shows and share any information they may have about the crimes and the suspects.

Notes

By middle school, your students have had years of instruction in decoding strategies, primarily in phonics, structural analysis, and context clues. Readers are taught these strategies to help them determine the meaning of words unfamiliar in print but known as part of their receptive vocabulary or to determine the meaning of totally unfamiliar words.

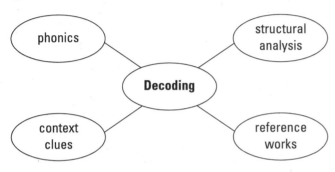

Phonics

Phonics is a system of teaching the basic sound-letter relationships in the English language. Many early grade educators believe phonics lays the foundation for young readers understanding the relationship between spoken and written words. Instruction is usually coupled with decodable text so that students can apply skills to predictable reading and develop *automaticity* — the ability to recognize words in text automatically and effortlessly. Good readers use phonics skills automatically in conjunction with other decoding strategies.

In the primary grades, phonics receives the main emphasis as a decoding strategy. The chart below shows when phonics instruction usually occurs.

Phonics	Grade When Taught
consonants (initial, medial, final)	through first half grade 2
consonant digraphs (/th/ *th*, etc.)	through first half grade 2
consonant clusters (*st, bl, br*, etc.)	through grade 2
short vowels	through grade 1
long vowels	through grade 2
r-controlled vowels (*er, ir, ar*, etc.)	through grade 2
diphthongs (*oi, oy*, etc.)	through grade 2
variant vowels (*ough, au, aw*, etc.)	through grade 2

As a result of phonics instruction, many young students can decode the vast majority of phonetically regular words they read. In the intermediate grades and beyond the problem becomes how to decode irregular and multisyllabic words that appear increasingly in reading materials.

Structural Analysis

Structural analysis is a strategy used to figure out the meaning of multisyllabic words. Students are taught to "chunk" words; that is, break words into recognizable parts based on syllabication rules or meaningful word parts.

Syllabication Rules Instruction and practice in syllabication rules helps students break words into smaller parts and then use phonics skills to pronounce the word. The following pages contain lessons devoted to teaching students these high-utility syllabication skills.

> **Rule 1:** When there are two consonants between two vowels, divide between the two consonants unless they are a blend or a digraph.
>
> **Rule 2:** When there are three consonants between two vowels, divide between the blend or the digraph and the other consonant.
>
> **Rule 3:** When there are two consonants between two vowels, divide between the two consonants between vowels unless they are a blend or a digraph. The first syllable is a closed syllable, and the vowel sound is short.
>
> **Rule 4:** Do not split common vowel clusters, such as vowel digraphs, r-controlled vowels, and vowel diphthongs.
>
> **Rule 5:** When you see a VCV pattern in the middle of a word, divide the word before or after the consonant. If you divide after the consonant, the first vowel sound is short. If you divide before the consonant, the first vowel sound is long.
>
> **Rule 6:** Divide compound words between the individual words.
>
> **Rule 7:** When a word includes an affix, divide between the base word and the affix (prefix or suffix).

When students use these syllabication rules to pronounce the word, they can match the word with a word already in their speaking vocabulary.

Meaningful Word Parts Another instructional strategy teaches students to look for meaningful word parts, beginning with the root or base word and moving on to prefixes and suffixes. Using knowledge of these parts, the reader assembles a meaning and attempts to match clues with words already in the speaking or receptive vocabulary. You can help your students use structural analysis by teaching the procedure outlined below.

> ## Example Sentence and Procedure
>
> His heart beat <u>thunderously</u>. There had been so many hope-filled moments before, all of them ending in bitter disappointment. (from "Zebra")
>
> 1. Find the root or base word and recall its meaning. (*thunder*)
> 2. Find the prefix and/or suffix and recall its meaning(s). (*-ous, -ly*)
> 3. Use the knowledge clues to predict the word's meaning. (*a sound like thunder*)
> 4. Check predicted meaning against the rest of the sentence. (*His heartbeat sounded like thunder.*)
> 5. Does the meaning make sense? (*yes*)

For additional suggestions on teaching structural analysis skills, see *The Language of Literature*.

Context Clues

Using context clues means using the knowledge provided by surrounding words and phrases to figure out the meaning of words. Students are taught to look for clues such as restatements, examples, comparisons, contrasts, definitions, and general descriptions. In addition to context clues, readers often use other decoding strategies.

You can help your students use context clues by teaching the procedure beneath the sample sentence.

> ## Example Sentence and Procedure
>
> In 1917 the United States entered World War I as an active <u>combatant</u>. Like many socially prominent women, Eleanor [Roosevelt] threw herself into the war effort. (from "Eleanor Roosevelt")
>
> 1. Look at the surrounding context for a description of the word or other clues.
> 2. Look at the word and apply other decoding strategies as necessary.
> 3. Use these clues to predict the word's pronunciation and meaning.
> 4. Check the predicted meaning against the rest of sentence.
> 5. Does the meaning make sense?

For additional suggestions on teaching context clues, see *The Language of Literature*.

Quick Diagnostic Test

Use the list below to determine how well your students read multisyllabic words. The lists are organized by syllabication rule. If your students are unable to read some or all of these words, teaching them high-utility syllabication rules may help improve their decoding skills. Use the lessons on the following pages to assist you.

(Rules 1, 3)	(Rule 5)
picture	model
happen	robot
feather	crazy
follow	never
usher	final

(Rule 2)	(Rule 6)
angler	whirlwind
merchant	grasshopper
tumbler	grapevine
children	wastebasket
purchase	earring

(Rule 4)	(Rule 7)
party	readjustment
poison	rebound
feature	childish
royal	unavoidable
chowder	unselfish

Lesson 1: Consonant Blends and Digraphs in Multisyllabic Words

This lesson will help students chunk, or syllabicate, multisyllabic words that contain consonant blends and digraphs. Your students most likely recognize blends and digraphs when they see them in print; however, they may have problems decoding multi-syllabic words if they attempt to syllabicate between the two letters in the blend or digraph. If you think your students would benefit from a review of blends and digraphs, begin with Parts 1 and 2. If not, you may go directly to Parts 3 and 4.

Part 1: Quick Review of Consonant Blends

Following are common consonant blends with examples of each. The two letters in each blend represent two sounds.

br	break, brand	sl	slick, slam
cr	crane, crack	ld	field, hold
dr	drive, drip	lk	milk
fr	free	lp	help
gr	green	lt	melt
pr	press	sc	scare
tr	true	sk	ski, risk
bl	blue	sm	smart
cl	clue, close	sn	snare, snack
fl	flame, flute	sp	spell, clasp
gl	glue, glide	st	state, twist
pl	please, plan	sw	switch, sway

DIRECT INSTRUCTION

To help your students focus on consonant blends, write the following sentences on the board.

> 1. <u>Brown</u> bears <u>slide</u> on the <u>frost</u>.
> 2. The <u>grand</u> <u>prize</u> was a <u>silk</u> <u>scarf</u>.
> 3. <u>Flutes</u> <u>fly</u> in <u>blue</u> <u>skies</u>.
> 4. <u>Sly</u> <u>smelt</u> <u>swim</u> in <u>swift</u> surf.

Ask a student read aloud the first sentence. Call attention to the words *brown, slide,* and *frost.*

You could say: What two letters do you see at the beginning of *brown (br),* at the beginning of *slide (sl),* and at the beginning and end of *frost (fr, st)?* These are called consonant blends. The consonant blends are made up of two consonant letters and stand for two sounds. You will always say both sounds when you sound out a word.

Follow the same procedure with the remaining sentences.

Answers: #2: grand (*gr*), prize (*pr*), silk (*lk*), scarf (*sc*); #3: Flutes (*fl*), fly (*fl*), blue (*bl*), skies (*sk*); #4: Sly (*sl*), smelt (*sm, -lt*), swim (*sw*), swift (*sw*)

Part 2: Quick Review of Consonant Digraphs

Following are consonant digraphs and examples of each. The two letters in each digraph represent one sound.

ch cheat, check, touch
sh shine, fish, push
th (voiced) that, the, this
th (voiceless) think, teeth, thumb, thank
wh (hw blend) where, whoops, when, white, wheel

DIRECT INSTRUCTION

Write these sentences on the board.

> 1. How <u>much</u> <u>fish</u> does a <u>whale</u> eat?
> 2. <u>She</u> will <u>think</u> <u>the</u> <u>thing</u> is <u>cheap</u>.
> 3. <u>When</u> will you <u>change</u> and <u>wash</u> <u>the</u> <u>sheets</u>?
> 4. Do <u>white</u> hens have <u>teeth</u>?

Ask a student to read aloud the first sentence.

You could say: What two letters do you see at the end of *much (ch),* at the end of *fish (sh),* and at the beginning of *whale (wh)?* The consonant digraphs are made up of two consonant letters but represent only one sound. You will say only one sound when you sound out a word.

Follow the same procedure with the remaining sentences.

Answers: #2: She (*sh*), think (*th*), the (*th*), thing (*th*), cheap (*ch*); #3: When (*wh*), change (*ch*), wash (*sh*), the (*th*), sheets (*sh*); #4: white (*wh*), teeth (*th*)

Part 3: Syllabication Strategy: Consonant Blends and Digraphs

In the following lesson, students will use their knowledge of consonant blends and digraphs to syllabicate words. You may find it helpful to review the most basic syllabication rule: *Each syllable has one and only one vowel sound.*

DIRECT INSTRUCTION

Write Rule 1 and the example words on the board or use the copymaster on page 48. Remind students that V stands for vowel and C stands for consonant. Ask a student to give examples of vowel and consonant letters.

> **Rule 1: VCCV**
> When there are two consonants between two vowels, divide between the two consonants unless they are a blend or a digraph.
>
> picture   happen   abrupt   feather

Have a student read Rule 1. Ask a student to explain the rule in his or her own words and then to read the first word.

You could say: Find the VCCV pattern in the word *picture (ictu)*. Do you see a blend or digraph? (no) Where would you divide this word according to Rule 1? (between the *c* and the *t*) Look at each syllable. Pronounce the word. Do you recognize the word?

Repeat the process with the remaining words.

Answers: hap/pen; a/brupt, feath/er

Write Rule 2 and the example words on the board or use the copymaster on page 48.

> **Rule 2: VCCCV**
> When there are three consonants between two vowels, divide between the blend or the digraph and the other consonant.
>
> angler   merchant   tumbler   children

Have a student read Rule 2. Ask a student to explain the rule in his or her own words and then to read the first word.

You could say: Find the VCCCV pattern in the word *angler (angle)*. Do you see a blend or digraph? (yes) Where would you divide this word according to Rule 2? (between the *n* and the *gl*) Look at each syllable. Pronounce the word. Do you recognize the word?

Repeat the process with the remaining words.

Answers: (mer/chant), (tum/bler), (chil/dren)

Part 4: Strategy Practice

Write the following words on the board. Have students divide the words according to the two rules, identify the rule, and pronounce the word.

Practice applying Rule 1

	Answers		Answers
scatter	scat/ter	whether	wheth/er
garden	gar/den	zipper	zip/per
crafty	craft/y	fashion	fash/ion
scarlet	scar/let	forget	for/get
traffic	traf/fic	respect	re/spect

Practice applying Rule 2

	Answers		Answers
hungry	hun/gry	nothing	noth/ing
concrete	con/crete	purchase	pur/chase
hundred	hun/dred	address	ad/dress
worship	wor/ship	supply	sup/ply
handsome	hand/some	employ	em/ploy

Cumulative practice

	Answers		Answers
written	writ/ten	toddler	tod/dler
constant	con/stant	lather	lath/er
secret	se/cret	sandal	san/dal
surplus	sur/plus	merchant	mer/chant
kindling	kin/dling	silver	sil/ver

Lesson 2: Short Vowels in Multisyllabic Words

When your students have trouble figuring out words unfamiliar in print, they are most likely having problems decoding the letters that stand for the vowel sound(s) in the word. Usually this is because the relationship between vowel sounds and letters that represent them isn't as predictable as the relationship between consonant sounds and the letters that represent them.

This lesson will help your students syllabicate words that contain short vowels. If you think your students would benefit from a review of short vowels, you may begin with Part 1. If not, skip directly to Parts 2 and 3.

Part 1: Quick Review of Short Vowels

Of the vowel sounds in English, the short vowels have the most predictable relationship between the sounds and the letters that represent them.

DIRECT INSTRUCTION

To help students focus on short vowels, write the list below on the board.

at	end	in	on	up
bat	bend	fin	odd	cup
and	vest	lick	mop	duck
fad	tell	drip	trot	lump

Have a student read the first column of words.

You could say: **What vowel sound do you hear in each of these words? (/a/ or short a) What letter represents that sound in each of these words? (the letter *a*).**

Follow the same procedure with the remaining lists.

Answers: column 2: /e/ or short e; column 3: /i/ or short i; column 4: /o/ or short o; column 5: /u/ or short u

Part 2: Syllabication Strategy: Short Vowels

Use the following syllabication strategy to help your students figure out some of the vowel sounds in multisyllabic words. You will note that Rule 3 expands upon Rule 1 introduced in Lesson 1.

DIRECT INSTRUCTION

Write Rule 3 and the example words on the board or use the copymaster on page 49. Remind students that V stands for vowel and C stands for consonant.

> **Rule 3: VCCV:**
> **When there are two consonants between two vowels, divide between the consonants unless they are a blend or a digraph. The first syllable is a closed syllable, and the vowel sound is short.**
>
> | butter | lather | follow | usher |
> |--------|--------|--------|-------|
> | summer | traffic | tender | invent |

Have a student read Rule 3 and explain the rule in his or her own words.

Have a student read the first word.

You could say: **Find the VCCV pattern in the word first word (*utte*). Do you see a blend or a digraph? (no) Where would you divide this word according to Rule 3? (between the two *t*'s) What vowel sound do you hear in the first syllable? (short) Look at each syllable and pronounce the word. Do you recognize the word?** Repeat this process with the remaining words.

Answers: lath/er, fol/low, ush/er, sum/mer, traf/fic, ten/der, in/vent

Part 3: Strategy Practice

Write the following on the board. Have students divide the words according to the rule and pronounce the word.

	Answers		Answers
under	un/der	billow	bil/low
bother	both/er	enter	en/ter
bottom	bot/tom	number	num/ber
rather	rath/er	object	ob/ject
practice	prac/tice	dipper	dip/per
snapper	snap/per	grammar	gram/mar
after	af/ter	sudden	sud/den
cashew	cash/ew	vintage	vin/tage
pencil	pen/cil	member	mem/ber

Lesson 3: Vowel Clusters in Multisyllabic Words

This lesson will show students how to chunk, or syllabicate, multisyllabic words that contain vowel clusters: long vowel digraphs, r-controlled vowels, and vowel diphthongs. If your students aren't aware of vowel clusters, they might syllabicate between the two vowels in the cluster. In that case, they will syllabicate incorrectly and mispronounce the word when they attempt to sound it out. If you think your students would benefit from a review of vowel clusters, begin with Parts 1-3. If not, skip to Parts 4 and 5.

Part 1: Quick Review of Long Vowel Digraphs

In words with vowel digraphs, two vowel letters are represented by one vowel sound.

DIRECT INSTRUCTION

Write the list below on the board.

cream	play	boat
beast	gray	coal
bean	paint	goat
green	aim	row
peel	stain	slow

Have a student read the first column of words.

You could say: What vowel sound do you hear in each of these words? (long e) What letters stand for the long e sound in *beast*? (*ea*) What letters stand for the long e sound in *green*? (*ee*) These are called vowel digraphs. Vowel digraphs are made up of two vowel letters that stand for one sound.

Follow the same procedure with the remaining lists.

Answers: column 2: long a, *ay* in *gray*, *ai* in *paint*; column 3: long o, *oa* in *boat*, *ow* in *slow*

Part 2: Quick Review of R-controlled Vowels

In words with r-controlled vowels, the vowel sound is influenced by the *r* that follows it.

DIRECT INSTRUCTION

Write the list below on the board.

fern	car	born
dirt	star	cord
fur	arm	sort
her	yarn	more
birth	farm	horn

Have a student read the first column of words.

You could say: These words all have the "er" sound. What letters stand for the "er" sound in *fur*? (*ur*) in *her*? (*er*) in *birth*? (*ir*) These are called r-controlled vowels. The r-controlled vowels are made up of a vowel and the letter *r*. In words with r-controlled vowels, the vowel sound is influenced by the *r* that follows it.

Follow the same procedure with the remaining columns.

Answers: column 2: all words have the ar sound; letters are *ar;* column 3: all words have the or sound; letters are *or.*

Part 3: Quick Review of Vowel Diphthongs

DIRECT INSTRUCTION

To help students focus on vowel diphthongs write this list on the board.

oil	ouch
boil	cloud
boy	how
spoil	scout
toy	towel

Have a student read the first column of words.

You could say: These words all have the oi sound. What letters stand for the oi sound in *boil* (*oi*) and in *boy*? (*oy*) These are called vowel diphthongs. Vowel diphthongs are made up of two vowel letters that stand for two vowel sounds.

Follow the same procedure with the remaining column.

Answers: column 2: all words have the ow sound; letters are *ou* or *ow.*

Part 4: Syllabication Strategy: Vowel Clusters

Use the following syllabication strategy to help your students syllabicate words that contain vowel clusters.

DIRECT INSTRUCTION

Write Rule 4 and the example words on the board or use the copymaster on page 49.

> **Rule 4:**
> Do not split common vowel clusters, such as long vowel digraphs, r-controlled vowels, and vowel diphthongs.
>
> party   poison   feature   royal   chowder   garden

Have a student read Rule 4. Have a student explain the rule in his or her own words.

Have a student read the first word.

You could say: Do you see a vowel cluster in this word? (yes) If you do, what is the cluster? (*ar*) Where would you avoid dividing this word according to Rule 4? (between the *a* and *r*) Where do you think you should divide the word? (after the cluster, between the *r* and *t*) Look at each syllable and pronounce the word. Do you recognize the word?

Repeat this process with the remaining words. In the case of *poison*, *feature*, and *royal*, students will be asked to syllabicate words for which they haven't learned all of the syllabication rules. Encourage them to try out what they know and attempt a pronunciation based on what they've learned so far.

Answers:

poison: (*oi*) avoid dividing between cluster; divide after the cluster

royal: (*oy*) avoid dividing between cluster; divide after the cluster

feature: (*ea*) avoid dividing between cluster; divide after the cluster

chowder (*ow*) avoid dividing between cluster; divide after the cluster

garden: (*ar*) avoid dividing between cluster; divide after the cluster

Part 5: Strategy Practice

Write the following on the board. Have students divide the words according to the rules they know, and pronounce the word.

	Answers		**Answers**
carton	car/ton	peanut	pea/nut
powder	pow/der	council	coun/cil
circus	cir/cus	purpose	pur/pose
mountain	moun/tain	moisture	mois/ture
maintain	main/tain	voyage	voy/age
fertile	fer/tile	mayor	may/or
darling	dar/ling	freedom	free/dom
coward	cow/ard	tailor	tai/lor
hornet	hor/net	eager	ea/ger
barter	bar/ter	order	or/der

Lesson 4: Short and Long Vowels in Multisyllabic Words

This lesson will help your students develop flexibility in applying syllabication strategies as they attempt to decode multisyllabic words.

Part 1: Quick Review

If you have skipped over Lessons 1-3, you may want to preview this lesson to be sure your students are prepared for more complicated syllabication strategy.

Part 2: Syllabication Strategy: Is the vowel sound long or short?

Use the following syllabication strategy to help your students decide whether a vowel letter stands for a long or short vowel sound.

DIRECT INSTRUCTION

Write Rule 5 and the example words on the board or use the copymaster on page 50. Remind students that V stands for vowel and C stands for consonant.

> **Rule 5: VCV:**
>
> **When you see a VCV pattern in the middle of a word, divide the word either before or after the consonant. If you divide the word after the consonant, the first vowel sound is short. If you divide the word before the consonant, the first vowel sound is long.**
>
> **model   robot   crazy   never**

Have a student read Rule 5 and explain the rule in his or her own words.

Ask a student to read the first word.

You could say: Find the VCV pattern in the first word. (*ode*) Where should you first divide the word? (after the *d*, the first consonant) What happens to the vowel sound in the first syllable? (The vowel sound is short.) Say the word. Do you recognize it? (yes) When the consonant is part of the first syllable, the first syllable is called "closed."

Ask a student to read the second word.

You could say: Find the VCV pattern in the second word. (*obo*) Where should you first divide the word? (after the *b*, the first consonant) What happens to the vowel sound in the first syllable? (The vowel sound is short.) Say the word. Do you recognize it? (no)

Try the second part of the rule. Where should you divide the word? (before the *b*, the first consonant) What happens to the vowel sound in the first syllable? (The vowel sound is long.) Say the word. Do you recognize it? (yes) When the consonant is part of the second syllable, the first syllable is called "open."

Repeat this process with the remaining words.

Answers: crazy: (*azy*) Divide after the *z*, the first consonant; vowel is short; no, do not recognize the word. Divide before the *z*; the vowel is long; yes, recognize the word.

never: (*eve*) Divide after the *v*; vowel sound is short; yes, recognize the word.

Part 3: Strategy Practice

Write the following words on the board. Have students divide the words and pronounce the word.

	Answers		Answers
legal	le/gal	final	fi/nal
gravel	grav/el	prefix	pre/fix
basic	ba/sic	level	lev/el
driven	driv/en	moment	mo/ment
minus	mi/nus	paper	pa/per
panic	pan/ic	soda	so/da
spider	spi/der	devil	dev/il
honor	hon/or	tiny	ti/ny
seven	sev/en		

Lesson 5: Compound Words

When students encounter multisyllabic words, they often don't try the obvious; that is, to look for words or word parts they already know within the longer word. Lessons 5 and 6 will help students develop these skills.

Part 1: Syllabication Strategy: Compound Words

Use the following syllabication strategy to help your students determine where to divide a compound word.

DIRECT INSTRUCTION ————————————

Write Rule 6 and the example words on the board or use the copymaster on page 50.

> **Rule 6:**
>
> **Divide compound words between the individual words.**
>
> grapevine   lifeguard   whirlwind
> butterfly   grasshopper

Have a student read Rule 6. Ask a student to explain the rule in his or her own words.

You could say: When you see a multisyllabic word, stop and see if it is made up of one or more words that you already know.

Have a student read the first word.

You could say: How many words do you see in the first word? (two) Where should you divide the word? (between *grape* and *vine*)

Repeat the process with the remaining words in the first row.

Answers: (life/guard), (whirl/wind)

Have a student read the first word in the second row.

You could say: How many words do you see in the word? (two) Where should you divide the word? (between *butter* and *fly*) Where else should you divide the word? (between the two *t*'s) How do you know? (Rule 1 says to divide two consonants between vowels.)

Repeat the process with the remaining words. (grass/hop/per)

Part 2: Strategy Practice

Write the following words on the board. Have students divide the words, identify the rule(s) they use, and pronounce the word.

	Answers		Answers
shipwreck	ship/wreck	buttermilk	but/ter/milk
postcard	post/card	notebook	note/book
screwdriver	screw/dri/ver	volleyball	vol/ley/ball
oatmeal	oat/meal	washcloth	wash/cloth
windmill	wind/mill	wastebasket	waste/bas/ket
dragonfly	dra/gon/fly	peppermint	pep/per/mint
pancake	pan/cake	hardware	hard/ware
earthquake	earth/quake	handlebar	han/dle/bar
pigtail	pig/tail	earring	ear/ring
wristwatch	wrist/ watch	weekend	week/end

Lesson 6: Affixes

This lesson will give students help in dividing multi-syllabic words that contain one or more affixes. These are the kinds of words that give students the most problems because they tend to be long and can look overwhelming. If you think your students would benefit from practice with identifying prefixes and suffixes, start with Parts 1 and 2. If not, go directly to Parts 3 and 4.

Part 1: Quick Review of Prefixes

Recognizing prefixes in multisyllabic words can help your students chunk words into manageable parts. You may use the following list of common prefixes and their meanings to expand upon the lesson described below.

auto-	self	by-	near, aside
mis-	bad	under-	below
pre-	before	un-	not, opposite of
re-	again, back	de-	reverse, remove from
with-	back, away	dis-	not, opposite
bi-	two	uni-	one
on-	on	be-	make
tri-	three		

DIRECT INSTRUCTION

Write the following prefixes and their meanings on the board.

auto-	self	bi-	two	un-	not

You could say: The word part on the left side of each pair is called a prefix. Prefixes can be added to root words or base words to change the meaning of the word. Think of a word that begins with this prefix.

Write the word on the board.

Follow the same procedure with the remaining prefixes. If you wish, include additional prefixes. Save the words and use them for syllabication practice later.

Possible answers: *auto-* (autobiography); *bi-* (bicycle, bifold,); *un-* (unhappy, unlikely)

Part 2: Quick Review of Suffixes

Recognizing suffixes in multisyllabic words can help your students chunk words into manageable parts. You may use the following list of common suffixes and their meanings to expand upon the lesson described below.

-ness	state or quality of	-less	without
-like	resembling	-ship	state or quality of
-ish	of, relating to	-ful	full of
-ways	manner	-er	one who
-ly	like, resembling	-ous	possessing, full of
-ion	act, condition	-ment	act, state of

DIRECT INSTRUCTION

Write the following suffixes and their meanings on the board.

-ness	state or quality of	-ly	resembling
-ful	full of		

You could say: The word part on the left side of each pair is called a suffix. When suffixes are added to root words or base words, they often change the part of speech of the root or base word. Think of a word that ends with this suffix.

Write the word on the board.

Follow the same procedure with the remaining suffixes. If you wish, include additional suffixes. Save the words and use them for syllabication practice later.

Possible answers: *-ness* (happiness, sadness); *-ly* (quickly, lively); *-ful* (thankful, eventful)

Part 3: Syllabication Strategy: Affixes

Use the following syllabication strategy to help your students determine where to divide words that contain affixes.

DIRECT INSTRUCTION

Write Rule 7 and the examples on the board or use the copymaster on page 50.

Rule 7:

When a word includes an affix, divide between the base word and the affix (prefix or suffix).

rebound	restless	unavoidable
preschool	childish	readjustment
disprove	joyous	unselfish

Ask a student read Rule 7 and to explain the rule in his or her own words.

Have a student read the first word in column 1.

You could say: **What prefix do you see in *rebound*? *(re)* Where should you divide *rebound* according to Rule 7? *(re/bound)* Continue with the remaining words in column 1. In each case, have students apply the rule, divide the word, pronounce the word, and then see if they recognize it.

Answers: pre/school; dis/prove

Have a student read the first word in column 2.

**What suffix do you see in *restless*? *(less)* Where should you divide *restless*? *(rest/less)* Continue with the remaining words in column 2. In each case, have students apply the rule, divide the word, pronounce the word, and then see if they recognize it.

Answers: child/ish; joy/ous

Have a student read the first word in column 3.

**What affixes do you see in this word? *(un, able)* Where should you divide the word? *(un/avoid/able)* Continue with the remaining words in column 3. In each case, have students apply the rule, divide the word, pronounce it, and then see if they recognize it. Note: In *avoid, a* is also considered a prefix, and *able* is considered a suffix. You can further divide the word as follows: un/a/void/a/ble.

Answers: re/adjust/ment and re/ad/just/ment; un/self/ish

If you wish to extend this lesson, have students analyze each word to see if they should apply additional syllabication rules.

Part 4: Strategy Practice

Write the following words on the board. Have students divide the words, identify the rule(s) they use, and pronounce the word.

Answers

uniform	uni/form (or u/ni/form)
fairly	fair/ly
beautiful	beau/ti/ful
unlikely	un/like/ly
recall	re/call
misfit	mis/fit
rigorous	rigor/ous (or rig/or/ous)
hopelessness	hope/less/ness
childlike	child/like
unwind	un/wind
opinion	opin/ion (and o/pin/ion)
hardship	hard/ship
sticker	stick/er
sideways	side/ways
department	de/part/ment
disbelieve	dis/believe (and dis/be/lieve)
withstand	with/stand
become	be/come
refreshment	re/fresh/ment

Name _____ Date _____

Rule 1: VCCV

When there are two consonants between two vowels, divide between the two consonants unless they are a blend or a digraph.

picture   happens   abrupt   feather

Rule 2: VCCCV

When there are three consonants between two vowels, divide between the blend or the digraph and the other consonant.

angler   merchant   tumbler   children

Name _____ Date _____

Rule 3: VCCV

When there are two consonants between two vowels, divide between the consonants unless they are a blend or a digraph. The first syllable is a closed syllable, and the vowel is short.

butter   lather   follow   usher
summer   traffic   tender   invent

Rule 4: Common Vowel Clusters

Do not split common vowel clusters, such as long vowel digraphs, r-controlled vowels, and vowel diphthongs.

party   poison   feature   royal
chowder garden

Name _____ Date _____

Rule 5: VCV

When you see a VCV pattern in the middle of a word, divide the word either before or after the consonant. If you divide the word after the consonant, the first vowel sound is short.
If you divide the word before the consonant, the first vowel sound is long.

model   robot   crazy   never

Rule 6: Compound Words

Divide compound words between the individual words.

grapevine   lifeguard   whirlwind
butterfly   grasshopper

Rule 7: Affixes

When a word includes an affix, divide between the baseword and the affix (prefix or suffix).

rebound   restless   unavoidable   preschool
childish   readjustment   disprove   joyous
unselfish

One of the reasons students struggle with reading comprehension is a failure to adjust their reading rate to their purpose. When students are asked to read difficult material or are unfamiliar with the structure of what they are reading, it often doesn't occur to them that they need to slow down their reading rate to comprehend the more difficult content.

Young readers are exposed primarily to narrative writing, usually in the form of fiction. Narrative fiction, often stories, comprises the majority of children's exposure to reading from the time they are able to thumb through a picture book to the time they can read an entire story independently. Because the story structure has become familiar over the years, students have certain expectations of the fictional narrative form. They anticipate finding most or all of the common elements that are in a basic story grammar, or outline: beginning, middle, end, setting, characters, events, conflict, and resolution.

As students advance grade levels, the scope of material they are asked to read broadens to include narrative nonfiction (social studies, biographies), informational material (textbooks and other instructional texts), poetry, and drama. These forms do not follow such a familiar narrative path. The content is more difficult, the structure less predictable, and the demand for retention increased. The combination of these elements may cause students to feel overwhelmed and outside their reading comfort zones.

Purposes for Reading

There are several techniques to help your students begin thinking about the relationship between rate and comprehension. First, however, it is important to make students aware that they read different types of material for different purposes. You might begin by asking the simple question:

"What is your purpose for reading?"

Three general answers to this question are:

- for enjoyment, for entertainment
- to learn, to be informed
- because I'm being tested on it

Reading for Enjoyment When we read for enjoyment, we naturally go at our own pace and fall into our own rhythm. This individualized speed is called our *independent reading level* (see page 3). For students to establish the practice of adjusting their own reading rate, they must first get a sense of their independent reading level, or the pace at which they read most comfortably. This will become the measure for adjusting the rate to a specific purpose when reading the wide variety of material required in middle school, high school, and beyond.

Encourage your students, the next time they are relaxing at home or have free time, to pick up a story or book of their choosing and read for enjoyment. Ask them to pay close attention to their reading rate. Tell them that they should be reading at the pace that allows them to best understand the text.

Reading for Information When students read to be informed, they have a focused objective—to gather information. This objective should have a bearing on how they approach the material. Once students have a sense of their rate when reading for enjoyment, you might ask, "How should your reading rate change when you read for information?" The answer most likely will be, "The reading rate slows down." However, the idea that rate changes with purpose does not always occur to students. They often read all types of material at the same rate, and will need to make a conscious effort to slow down. Even though this skill may not feel natural at first, it will better enable students to absorb, process, and understand more complex and difficult content.

Reading for Assessment This may be the most demanding type of reading and the most difficult purpose to adjust to. When students read for assessment, they are usually being timed and are acutely aware that every wrong answer will count against them. Students may assume that because they are taking a timed test they should read faster. Tell students they can fight test anxiety by making a conscious effort to slow down their reading and thereby increase their level of comprehension. For more information about reading for assessment, check the Reading and Writing for Assessment feature in the Unit Wrap-Up section in *The Language of Literature*.

Reading Techniques for Informational Material

Skimming for an Overview You may think of this technique for helping students adjust reading rate as "guided skimming." The purpose is to provide students with an overview of difficult material prior to reading. Have students skim the material while you bring key information to their attention. By providing an overview, this exercise sets up similar pre-reading assistance for the reading of nonfiction as a story grammar does for the reading of fiction.

1. Ask students to skim the material in their books as you point out the basic structure, including the chapter title, the introduction, the body of the text, and the conclusion.

2. Begin again, this time indicating subheads, key words and phrases, pronunciation guides, margin information, maps, timelines, and diagrams and other graphics as they appear.

3. As you point out each feature, ask students why they think it appears on the page. For example, a timeline might represent the period from 2000 to 500 B.C., when the early Greeks inhabited the Aegean Sea region. You could ask students why they think a timeline is included on this page. One answer might be that the timeline offers another way to "see" the time in history that the chapter is addressing.

4. Once you have been through the passage once or twice doing guided skimming, ask students how the exercise affected their reading rate. Did skimming make them read slower or faster? In some cases, students may read faster because there is less material to comprehend. In other cases, focusing on the elements of an overview might cause students to slow down, because they are trying to synthesize information.

Students should understand that timelines and other features are placed on the page to provide background information on the subject and to help guide, support, and further explain the text. You can help students learn how to use these items as tools for understanding difficult material and monitoring their reading rate.

Turning Subheads into Questions Subheads introduce sections and parts of chapters. They can also serve as a pre-reading strategy and provide a purpose for reading. At the beginning of each section, read (or have a student read) each subhead aloud. Then ask a student to turn the subheads into ques-

tions. For example, if the first subhead in the chapter reads "The Early Greeks," the student should formulate the question: Who were the early Greeks? If the second subhead reads "The Land Around the Sea," the question would be: What (and/or where) is the land around the sea?

Knowing they will have to answer these questions when they are finished with the passage helps students find a specific purpose for reading. After students have given their answers, you can ask for comments on how looking for answers helped with comprehension and affected students' reading rate. Any subhead can be turned into a question, and this is a technique students can learn to do independently.

Summarizing After reading a passage, a student should be able to restate the main idea of a passage in his or her own words. Tell students that they will be expected to give a summary of a passage you choose once they are finished reading it. When they are finished, ask a few students to give a brief summary. You could ask:

- Did knowing you would have to summarize change your reading rate?

- Did you slow down? speed up? maintain the same rate?

- How do you think your reading rate affected your comprehension?

The desired effect is a closer read of the material and extra attention to details. If students are struggling with their summaries, ask them to make rate adjustments and try reading the passage again.

There may be a host of reasons students struggle to understand what they read. Failure to adjust their reading rate to the purpose could be an important reason. Because many readers were brought up reading for enjoyment, making deliberate changes to a long-practiced reading style may not come naturally. It is an acquired skill. However, it may be first a matter of making students aware that they are able to change their reading style, and second, guiding them in the discovery that it is not only possible, but necessary. Helping students adjust their reading rate to their purpose could unlock the door to greater reading comprehension for many students.